THE STORM

W9-CAA-891

FIELD TRANSLATION SERIES 1

Eugenio Montale

THE STORM
AND OTHER POEMS

Translated by
Charles Wright

With an Introduction by Vinio Rossi

FIELD Translation Series 1

Some of these translations first appeared in
Chelsea and *Granite*, and in *The Selected Poems of
Eugenio Montale*, published in 1965 by New Direc-
tions.

Grateful acknowledgment is made to the
American-Italian Fulbright Commission, and
especially to Cipriana Scelba, for a student grant
during the years 1963-65, the period in which
these translations were made.

Publication of this book was made possible
through a grant from the Ohio Arts Council.

Library of Congress Cataloging in Publication Data
  Montale, Eugenio (translated by Charles Wright)
    The Storm and other poems

  LC: 78-67993
  ISBN: 0-932440-00-2
  0-932440-01-0 (paperback)

CONTENTS

9   Introduction

     I
     FINISTERRE

23   The Storm
25   Seaside
26   On a Letter Never Written
27   In Sleep
28   Indian Serenade
30   The Earrings
31   The Strands of Hair
32   Fiesole Window
33   The Red Lily
35   The Fan
36   Personae Separatae
38   The Ark
40   Day and Night
42   Your Flight
44   To My Mother

II
AFTERWARDS

49   Florentine Madrigals
51   From a Tower
53   Ballad Written in a Clinic

III
INTERLUDE

59   Two in Twilight
62   Where the Tennis Court Was . . .
66   Visit to Fadin

IV
FLASHES AND DEDICATIONS

71   Towards Siena
72   On the Greve
73   The Black Trout
74   A Metropolitan Christmas
75   Freeing a 'Dove'
76   Argyll Tour
78   Wind on the Crescent
79   On the Highest Column
81   Towards Finisterre
82   On the Llobregat
83   From the Train
84   Syria
85   Winter Light
87   For an 'Homage to Rimbaud'
88   Spellbound

V
SILVAE

91   Iris
94   In the Greenhouse
96   In the Park
98   The Orchard
101 Beach at Versilia
104 Ezekiel Saw the Wheel
106 Hitler Spring
109 Voice Arriving With the Coots
112 The Shadow of the Magnolia
114 The Lemon-Yellow Rooster
116 The Eel

VI
PRIVATE MADRIGALS

121 The Processions of 1949
123 Magenta-Colored Clouds
125 For an Album
127 From a Swiss Lake
129 Anniversary

VII
TEMPORARY CONCLUSIONS

133 Little Testament
135 The Prisoner's Dream

139 Notes

INTRODUCTION

by Vinio Rossi

The position held by Eugenio Montale's *La Bufera e altro* (*The Storm and other poems*, 1956) among contemporary collections of poetry is not difficult to assess. In its sweep over the spread of human experience and in its technical perfection it brings to mind other milestones of twentieth-century poetry: Eliot's *Four Quartets*, Valéry's "Cimetière marin," Yeats's *The Tower*, Rilke's *Duineser Elegien*. It seems to me now more than time enough that English readers have at their disposal the major collection of the 1975 Nobel laureate's poems in the version of a poet and translator of the quality of Charles Wright.

Although Montale considered *La Bufera* his best book, he never meant to disparage his two earlier collections, *Ossi di Seppia* (*Cuttlefish Bones*, 1925), and *Le Occasioni* (*The Occasions*, 1939). Indeed, he felt you couldn't really enter into *La Bufera* without having first immersed yourself in the land-scapes that preceded it. Actually, "seascape" would be the more appropriate term: in *Ossi* and later in *Le Occasioni* Montale's vision and experience, his sense of not adhering to reality, all seemed drawn to, and absorbed by, the ocean. "Later I understood that the sea was everywhere; even the classical architecture of the Tuscan hills was for me movement and flight." In both earlier books, moreover, Montale tries to span the chasm between external and internal worlds, "while carving out a new dimension in our ponderous polysyllabic language which would not brook an experience like mine"; in striving to attain an "essential language," he would wring the neck of eloquence even at the risk of counter-eloquence.

In exploring the powers inherent in the language of things and that language's musicality, Montale suggests two predecessors: Mallarmé (the external world exists only to reveal our inner states), and T. S. Eliot (the world presents a fund of objective signs that synthesize the expression of feelings); yet Montale's artistic development was in no way plotted according to an *a priori* esthetic program. It was, rather, intuitive, musical, and responsive only to internal exigencies. Typical of this mode is a lyric written when Montale was barely twenty:

> To spend the afternoon, absorbed and pale
> beside a burning garden wall,
> hearing, among the stubble and the thorns,
> the blackbirds cackling and the rustling snakes.
>
> On the cracked earth or in the vetch
> to spy on columns of red ants
> now crossing, now dispersing,
> atop their miniature heaps.
>
> To ponder, peering through the leaves,
> the heaving of the scaly sea
> while the cicadas' wavering screech
> rises from balding peaks.
>
> And, walking out into the sunlight's glare,
> to feel with melancholy wonder
> how all of life and its travail
> is in this following a wall
> lined with the shards of broken bottles.

Montale's tone, already present in this early poem, is one that evokes extreme desolation in an "existential" landscape. Liguria's coastline, just south of Genoa, with its rough, lean, hallucinating beauty, stamped its image upon the poet's youthful sensibilities. The very same landscape also prompted the more open, more experimental mode of his early work:

> But the illusion fails and time recalls us
> to noisy cities where the sky appears
> only in snatches, beyond the cornices.
> Rain wearies the earth; winter's
> tedium thickens upon the houses,
> light grows stingy, the soul goes bitter.
> And then, one day, through a half-shut gate,
> the yellow lemons catch our eye
> and the heart's frost thaws
> while somewhere within us songs
> begin to shower
> from golden trumpets of sunlight.
>
> (from "Lemons," *Ossi di Seppia*)

Le Occasioni, lyrics written during his twenty-year Tuscan period, continue his explorations in "rough and essential" language. Romantic effusions yield to a more objective expression, a tighter weave of rhyme, rhythm, and assonance. Montale himself says he was trying to find his own version of Gerard Manley Hopkins' "sprung rhythm."

The second volume differs from *Ossi* in that the majority of the lyrics are more immediately anchored in the incidents of a personal and private narrative. The familiar, second-person "tu" of the lead poem is the female figure that appears throughout the subsequent volumes. Montale was later to twit his critics in the very first poem of *Satura* (1971):

> Misled by me
> the critics assert that my "tu"
> is an institution, that were it not
> for this fault of mine, they'd have known
> that the many in me are one,
> even though multiplied by the mirrors.
> The trouble is that once caught in the net
> the bird doesn't know if he is himself
> or one of his too many duplicates.
>
> (The Use of "Tu")

Whether "cloud or woman, angel or stormy petrel," the "tu" is so compressed by allusive detail, so enriched by the "start of memory" (see below, p. 111), that it functions like the principal note, evoking in sympathetic vibration any number of simultaneous overtones. The feminine referent thus lives in the emotionally charged universe of the imagination.

The "Motets," in particular, a suite of

twenty poems embedded in *Le Occasioni*, have been said to be the most hermetic poems Montale ever wrote. And yet through various readings and the associative thinking they foster, their seal has slowly given way, signs have emerged with greater clarity, and a coherent thread of association has assumed its contours. Through it all a strong, familiar voice is heard, intimately addressing an absent "tu."

The missing wedge of the orange, or lemon, as Montale described it in speaking of *Le Occasioni*, was "their pedal of profound music, of contemplation," and it found expression in the poems written during 1940-42 and published in 1943 under the title *Finisterre*. These lyrics, the first section of *La Bufera*, complete the work of *Le Occasioni* by placing the female figure against a backdrop of terrestrial and cosmic war, by giving voice to the poet's historical and human condition. The title of the *plaquette* alone, *Finisterre*, land's end, suggests Montale's feelings of isolation at the time. Dismissed under Fascist pressure, for "political deficiencies," from his director's post at the Vieusseux library, he remained in Florence until well after the war. The epigraph too — from Agrippa d'Aubigné's first section ("Les Misères"), of *Les Tragiques* (1616), in which the Protestant poet, in a France torn by religious strife, complains to God of the indifference of war-lords — was enough to antagonize any Fascist censor and to urge publication in Switzerland.

The remaining lyrics of *La Bufera* were written in the last years of the war and during the early post-war period; they were ultimately published, along with the "Finisterre" series, in 1956 under the title of the series' lead poem. The post-war lyrics, whose inspiration was, as Montale says, more immediate, seem to represent a return to the impressionism and the greater directness of *Ossi*, but filtered through a more deliberate stylistic control. Along with a loosening of the mesh of images, whose texture, Montale thought, was far too tight in the earlier volumes, their interplay also relaxed, and leaps of association became more breathtaking. The feminine figure, though, remained unchanged; whether visiting angel, Muse, Iris, Clizia, nightingale, or lover, she always has her roots in the real world. Even

as image, she discards her earthly attributes
with great reluctance (see below, "Magenta-
Colored Clouds," page 123). But in the
slow and unconscious process of transform-
ing into an image, a poetic nucleus, she
often sheds her human and physical im-
mediacy to attract clusters of associative
images, which agglutinate around her. She
is consequently evoked "as absence, as
sorrow, as vague and phantasmic apparitions,
or that tiny bit of presence that becomes,
for him who receives her, a memento, an
admonition."

Against the rumble of war she is primarily
absence, however, an absence that becomes
a premonition of death (see especially "Bal-
lad Written in a Clinic," page 53). In this
way, Montale connects with the tradition of
the love lyric of the Troubadours, and of
Dante and Petrarch. But in his language
Montale is closer to the rough and gritty
rhymes and hard-edged images of Dante
(especially the Dante of the *Rime petrose*),
than to the elegant and courtly expression of
Petrarch's sonnets.

Montale owes his stature in Italian poetry
mainly to his success in dusting off old

rhythmic and imagistic models and recasting them with modern sensibility. He returns to an older, pristine tradition when language and its literary forms were fresh and vibrant. Among the first to break away from the official literary language of Italy, he avoided the rhetoric of D'Annunzio and Pascoli, the whimpers and whispers of the Crepuscularists. Those poets had, it is true, initiated a search for a poetic vocabulary that was not an end in itself but rather a means of communicating an intangible internal world. But except for Leopardi, there had not been a poet since Petrarch whose poetic vocabulary succeeded in correlating the outer and inner worlds of the poet. The Crepuscularists, especially Corazzini and Gozzano, with their emphasis on the ordinary and their blend of conversational and traditional language, took great steps in this direction. It was, however, the Hermetic poets, Ungaretti, Montale, Campana, who overthrew the rhetorical tradition by making the image the basic unit of their vocabulary and by weaving objects into a poetic fabric that creates a world of its own.

In 1940 Eugenio Montale said that the new

and difficult poet is one "who works with his own poem as though it were an object, accumulating in it, by instinct, meanings and echoes; conciliating in it the irreconcilable, making of it the most solid, unique, and precise correlative of his own inner experience." His tendency "is towards the object, towards an art clothed with, and incarnated in, the expressive medium, towards a passion that has become a *thing*. . . . Only when it has reached this stage does poetry exist; and it leaves an echo, an obsession of itself."

Montale presents a voice, unmistakable even in his prose pieces, even in his discarded lyrics. His vocabulary of images, mostly drawn from his native Cinque Terre in Liguria, bears the Montalian imprint: the hard, rocky, furrowed shoreline, the flux and friction of the ebb tide, tempests, squalls, gales and storms, sunflowers and lemon blossoms. These, together with enlarged syntactical possibilities and harsh sonorities, are indeed the cadences of Montale's harmonics.

One last remark. "La bufera" of the volume was a dialect term introduced into the literary idiom by Dante. It signifies a high wind with precipitation; figuratively, the word suggests upheaval and is frequently used to suggest the effects of passion. "Bufera," then, has a literary resonance much like "tempest" in English. In Canto V:31 of the *Inferno*, Dante uses "la bufera infernal" to describe the winds that perpetually drive flocks of lovers.

Oberlin, 1978

NOTES

The text used is an early edition of Mondadori's "Specchio" poetry series. In subsequent editions, Montale added a sixth poem to the five "Private Madrigals," "Se t'hanno assomigliato."

The phrase "rough and essential" I apply to the language Montale was striving to attain comes from the seventh in the Mediterranean cycle of *Ossi di Seppia*.

The English versions from *Ossi* were rendered by David Young; "The Use of 'Tu'" from *New Poems*, trans. by G. Singh (New York, New Directions, 1976).

I have translated the prose passages from Montale's introduction to *E. M., Poesie*, trans. by Gösta Andersson (Stockholm-Rome, Italica, 1960); from *Intenzioni* (*Intervista immaginaria*), published in *La Rassegna d'Italia* I (January, 1946), 84-89, collected in E.M., *Sulla Poesia*, ed. Giorgio Zampa (Mondadori, Milan, 1976), 561-69, also translated by Jonathan Galassi and published in a special number devoted to Montale of *Pequod*, II (Winter, 1977), 43-50.

Especially useful to me have been remarks about translating Montale by Charles Wright, made during a stay at Oberlin in November, 1976 and published in *Field*, No. 17 (Fall, 1977).

The everyday world serves as a springboard for both Dante and Montale, but their concerns transcend by far their historical and geographical reality. Dante's presence is pervasive in *La Bufera*, and it is fitting that it be noted explicitly. The lyric attributed to Dante and used as epigraph to "Hitler Spring" speaks of Clizia, who was changed into a Heliotrope (sunflower, "girasole"), and who symbolized constancy in love.

FINISTERRE

THE STORM

Les princes n'ont point d'yeux pour voir ces grand's merveilles,
Leurs mains ne servent plus qu'à nous persécuter . . .

(*Agrippa D'Aubigné: À Dieu*)

The storm that trickles its long March
thunderclaps, its hail, onto the stiff
leaves of the magnolia tree;

(sounds of shaking crystal which startle you
in your nest of sleep; and the gold
snuffed on the mahogany, on the backs
of the bound books, flares again
like a grain of sugar in the shell
of your eyelids)

the lightning that blanches
the trees and walls, freezing them
like images on a negative (a benediction
and destruction you carry carved
within you, a condemnation that binds you
stronger to me than any love, my strange sister);
and then the tearing crash, the jangling sistrums, the
    rustle
of tambourines in the dark ditch of the night,
the tramp, scrape, jump of the fandango . . . and
    overhead
some gesture that blindly is groping . . .

                    as when

turning around, and, sweeping clear your forehead
of its cloud of hair,

you waved to me — and entered the dark.

SEASIDE

The air rattles, the darkness is torn to shreds,
and the shadow you threw along the fragile
palisade curls up.   Too late in the day

if you want to be yourself! The rat plops
from the palm, the lightning is on the fuse,
is on the long, long lashes of your look.

ON A LETTER NEVER WRITTEN

Today, do the paired dolphins
leap with their children
for the swarming dawns, for the few
threads that catch
the fluff of life and bind themselves
into hours, into years? O, let me hear
no further word of you; let me escape the lightning-
    flash
of your eyes.   There are other things on this earth.

But I don't know how to run away, or run back; the
    night's
vermilion forge starts late; the evening lengthens;
praying is anguish and,
among the rising, knife-edged rocks, the bottle
has not yet reached you from the sea.   The wave,
    empty,
breaks on the point, at Finisterre.

IN SLEEP

The cries of owls, or the intermittent heartbeats
of dying butterflies,
or the moans and sighs
of the young, or the error that tightens
like a garrote around the temples, or the vague horror
of cedars uprooted by the onrush of night — all this
can come back to me, overflowing from ditches,
bursting from waterpipes, and awaken me
to your voice. The music of a slow, demented dance
cuts through; the enemy clangs down
his visor, hiding his face. The amaranth moon
enters behind the closed eyelids, becomes a swelling
cloud; and when sleep takes it
deeper in, it is still blood beyond any death.

INDIAN SERENADE

Still, this is ours, this shredding away of the evenings;
and ours this light-blade which rises from the sea
into the gardens, wounding the aloe.

You can lead me by the hand, if you pretend
you're with me, if I'm foolish enough

to follow for long, if that which leads me,

that which you say, seems in your power.

*   *   *

Were it your life which held me
on the doorsteps — and I could lend you a face,
become delirious.   But it's not,

it's not like that.   The octopus that slides
his inky fingers among the reefs
can use you.   You belong to him

and don't know it.   You *are* him, and think you are
    yourself.

THE EARRINGS

The lamp-black of the mirror does not preserve
the shadows of absences. (And of yours there is no
    trace.)
The sponge has already passed which scatters,
defenseless, the glitterings from the circle of gold.
I have searched for the stones, for the corals,
for the great force that carries you off. I flee
the unincarnate goddess; I carry
my longings until, at your light, they are consumed.
Elytra hum outside; the mad burial
is humming and knows that two lives don't count.
In the mirror's frame the soft
jellyfish of the evening appear. Your image
will come from the earth, however — where, at your
    earlobes,
squalid hands, turned over, hold the corals.

THE STRANDS OF HAIR . . .

You mustn't push back the bangs which veil
your child-like forehead. They, too, speak
of you — they are the whole sky wherever I go,
my only light except for the jades
which circle your wrist, in the riot
of sleep the curtains which
your amnesties drop; they carry you,
transmigratory Artemis, unharmed
among the wars of the still-born; and, if now
hair light as down flowers
upon that brow, you, leapt down from some height,
alter its color, your restless forehead
merges with dawn, and hides it.

FIESOLE WINDOW

Here where the unrelenting cricket bores
through silk clothes,
and the odor of camphor fails to rout
the moths that turn to dust in the books,
a bird, in spirals, swings
up to the elm tree where the sun
is trapped among darkened foliage.
Another light that does not brim,
other flashes, O my scarlet ivies.

THE RED LILY

If one day the red lily
should take root in your twenty-year-old heart
(The catch-basin sparkled among the rock-sieves of
the fishermen; glistening water rats splashed
in the cane brakes; towers
and banners beat out against the rain;
and the graft, taking hold in the new sun,
unknown to you, was finished);

the red lily already sacrificed
to the mistletoe
on the far crags, tearing at your scarf,
your hands, with an incorruptible ice, —
ditch flower which, in you, will open
upon the dark banks where the hubbub
of time no longer jangles . . . : to strike
the celestial harp, to make death, for you, a friend.

THE FAN

Ut Pictura . . . The disconcerting lips,
The glances, signals, the days now fallen wide;
I try to fix them there, as though enframed
By looking backward through a telescope,
Mute, still, but more alive. It was a joust
Of men and arms in flight among that smoke
The east wind struck, which dawn had long since
    reddened,
Trembling at first, then breaking through the mist.
The mother-of-pearl brightens, the rutted earth,
Vertiginous, gulps down its other victims;
But your stiff feathers against those cheeks grow pale,
And the day, perhaps, is safe. O heavy blows,
When you expand, O cruel flashes, O thunder
Upon the crowds! (Must he who knows you die?)

PERSONAE SEPARATAE

Like some golden scale which surfaces
from the dark and liquid distance and drips
over the corridor
of the skeletal carob trees, are we, too, *personae separatae*
always to the eyes of others? The word is a small thing;
also a small thing is the space in this crude
and cloudy sky, dark between moons: what is missing,
what twists the heart and makes me late here
among the trees, waiting for you, is a lost
meaning, or the fire, if you wish, which prints, on the
     ground,
the new trunks of the trees into parallel outlines,
concordant shadows, hands

of a single quadrant, and, too, brims the pitted
stumps, nest-hills for ants. The human wood
is over-cut, the yearly voice
too hollow, too restive
the mountain gap flaking to powder
under the snow-covered ridges of Lunigiana. Your
    shadow
passed by here, rested a moment on the rope pile
among the dried-out weirs, then loosened
like a breath around us — and here
there was no surging dread, in you the light
still found out light. But no longer. Now, at dawn,
    night
already is half-way down.

THE ARK

The umbrella of the willow tree
turns upside-down in the spring storm;
in April's whirlwind
the golden fleece hiding my dead ones,
my faithful dogs, my old servants,
becomes entangled in the garden — how many of them
  since then
(when the willow was golden and I would break
its fingers with my sling-shot) have fallen,

still living, into the trap. Surely the storm
will bring them together under
that earlier roof, but far away, farther away
than this lightning-sliced earth
where lime and blood seethe in the imprint
of the human foot. The soup-ladle smokes
in the kitchen, its round, reflecting lens
focusing the lean faces, the pointed muzzles,
and will protect them under the magnolia tree
if a gust of wind blows them there   The spring storm
stirs my ark like the yelp of a faithful dog,
O memories lost in me.

DAY AND NIGHT

Even a driving feather could sketch
your face, or a sun's ray playing hide-and-seek
over the woodwork, or bouncing back
from a child's mirror, or from the roofs. Along the
    stone walls
skeins of vapor stretch the church spires
of the poplars while down below the knife-grinder's
    parrot

squawks on his perch.   And then the sultry, hanging
    night
over the square, over the footsteps; and always this flat
exhaustion of daily going down only to come up again;
    nightmares
that cannot rediscover the light of your eyes
in the incandescent cave — and still the same yowls,
the same weeping on the veranda,
if suddenly the shot echoes which reddens
your throat, breaks your wings, stripping your feathers,
O perilous messenger of the dawn,
making cloisters and hospitals reveille
to a blast of trumpets . . .

YOUR FLIGHT

Two lights will wrangle over your soul
at the ditch which slides under
the dome of the thorn trees
if you appear in the flame (they dangle
from your bangs and stick like stars
in your amulets).

Your dress is in tatters, the trampled
shrubs spring back up,

and the swollen fish pond of the human condition,
choked with tadpoles, opens upon the furrows of the
   night.

Don't stir up the filthy
edges; leave
the burning wood-heaps untouched, the smoke
still strong, and clinging to the survivors!

If you gutter the flame (the hair
ash-blonde upon
that delicate wrinkle the sky
has abandoned)
how will the hand, bearer of silks
and precious stones, recover, ever again,
its faithful one from among the dead?

TO MY MOTHER

Now that the chorus of the rock partridge
lulls you in the eternal sleep and the gay,
broken band is in flight toward the hills
of Mesco, long picked clean of their harvest; now that
   the struggle
of the living rages even stronger, if you yield up,
like a shadow, your last remains
        (and it isn't a shadow,
dear, gentle soul, it isn't what you think)

who will protect you? The cleared highway
is not a passage; only two hands, a face,
those hands, *that* face, the gestures of a life
that is no other, that is nothing but itself —
only this puts you into the heaven
full of the souls and voices in which you live;

and the question you leave unanswered is also
only one of your gestures in the shadow of the crosses.

II

AFTERWARDS

FLORENTINE MADRIGALS

11 September 1943

Shut out, Herma, with tape and sealing wax,
the vain, unveiling hope
so lately seen again in your mornings.
On the wall where we once read
DEATH TO BIG MOUSTACHE THE QUEER they
slap on another coat of paint.   Up there a vagabond
loosens hand-bills over the clouded
courtyard.   And the drone dwindles away.

A Bedlington sticks his face out like a small,
blue sheep where those stumps
— *Trinity Bridge* — quiver across the water. If yesterday's
(and tomorrow's) overlords go down
like sewer rats, the blows that hammer
against your temples as far away as the hospital wards
of Paradise are still the gong
that calls you back among us, O my sister.

FROM A TOWER

I have seen the black water bird
cut down from the lightning rod:
I knew him by his prideful flight,
by his roulade of notes.

I have seen the long-eared and festive
Piquillo shoot up from the tombstone

and, by fits and starts, with a moist trumpet
of scales, reach the roof.

I have seen, in the stained-glass windows,
through the flowers of the mullioned panes,
a country of skeletons
filter in — and a lip
of blood grow muter, speechless.

BALLAD WRITTEN IN A CLINIC

In the wake of the emergency:

when the mad August comet
burst over the mountains
in the still-serene air

— but bringing darkness for us, and terror,
and crumbling roof eaves and crumbling bridges
falling upon us, we like Jonah buried
in the guts of the whale —

and I turned around and the mirror
of myself was no longer
the same because they had shut up, suddenly,
your throat and your chest
in a plaster mannequin.

In the pit of your eye-sockets
bright lenses of tears shone
thicker than these huge
tortoise-shell glasses of yours
which I take from you at night and place
next to the phial of morphine.

The god Taurus was never ours;
ours was the god who touches
the spring ditch lilies with flame:
Ariete I invoked, and the flight
of the horned monster knocked over,
with his last, vainglorious kick,
even the heart wrenched by your coughs.
I wait for a sign if it's the time
for the last abduction:

I am ready and the penance
starts even now in the dark sob
of the valleys and the ravines
of the *other* Emergency.

You've put the wooden bulldog
on the nightstand, the clock
with the luminous hands
which spills watery light
over your fitful sleep,

the nothing that satisfied
whomever would force the narrow gate;
and outside, and raised, deep red
bleeds a cross against the white.

I turn my face with yours toward the voice
which breaks through in the dawn, to the enormous
presence of the dead; and then the howl

of the wooden dog is my own, and soundless.

III
INTERLUDE

TWO IN TWILIGHT

A watery brightness flows between you and me
here on the belvedere, distorting the profiles of the hill,
and distorting your face.
It plays across a flickering background, cuts off
from you your every gesture; comes on without a trace,
and leaves in a way that fills in every track, closing
over your footsteps:

you here with me, inside this fallen air,
it seals up
the numbness of boulders.
                            And I turn back
from this force which weighs down around us, give in
to the witchcraft of recognizing nothing
in me that is outside myself: if I raise
my arm even an inch, the act
makes me something I'm not, it shatters against glass,
    its memory
unknown and shadowed over, and the gesture
no longer belongs to me;
if I speak, I listen to an astonished voice
descending to its farthest range,
or wasted, now, in the unsustaining air.

Thus, to the point that it resists until the last
wasting away of the afternoon,
this bewilderment goes on; then a gust of wind
lifts up the valleys again in a frenzied
jerking, and a tinkling sound
drifts from the foliage which scatters
in a fast-running smoke, and the first lights
sketch in the quays.

                                    . . . the words
drop lightly between us. I look at you

in the quivering dusk.   I'm not sure
that I know you; I *do* know that I was never so far apart
from you as now, in this late returning.
These few moments have burned away
everything of us: except for two faces, two masks
which carve on their surfaces, with difficulty,
two smiles.

WHERE THE TENNIS COURT WAS . . .

Where the tennis court once was, enclosed
by the small rectangle down by the rail-
road tracks where the wild pines grow, the
couch-weed now runs matted over the
ground, and the rabbits scratch in the tall
grass in those hours when it is safe to
come out.

One day here two sisters came to play, two
white butterflies, in the early hours of the
afternoon. Toward the east the view was
(and still is) open — and the damp rocks
of the Corone still ripen the strong grapes
for the 'sciacchetra.' It is curious to think
that each of us has a country like this one,

even if altogether different, which must always remain *his* landscape, unchanging; it is curious that the physical order of things is so slow to filter down into us, and then so impossible to drain back out. But what of the rest? Actually, to ask the how and why of the interrupted game is like asking the how and why of that scarf of vapor rising from the loaded cargo ship anchored down there at the docks of Palmaria. Soon they will light, in the gulf, the first lamps.

Around, as far as the eye can see, the iniquity of objects persists, intangibly. The grotto encrusted with shells should be unchanged in the dense and heavy-planted garden under the tennis court; but the fanatical uncle will come no more with his tripod camera and magnesium lamp to photograph the single flower, unrepeatable, risen from the spiny cactus, and pre-destined to live only the shortest of lives. Even the villas of the South Americans seem deserted. And there haven't always been the heirs and heiresses ready to squander their sumptuously shoddy goods

that came always side-by-side with the
rattle of pesos and milreis. Or maybe the
sarabande of the newly arrived tells us of
passings on to other regions: surely we
here are perfectly sheltered and out of the
line of fire. It is almost as though life
could not be ignited here except by light-
ning; as though it feeds only on such inert
things as it can safely accumulate; as
though it quickly cankers in such deserted
zones.

'*Del salon en el angulo oscuro — silenciosa y
cubierta de polvo — veiase el arpa . . .*' Oh,
yes, the museum would be impressive if
one were able to uncover this ex-paradise
of Victoriana. And no one was ever seen
again on the seashell-inlayed terrace, sup-
ported by the giant Neptune (now scraped
clean) after the Lion of Callao lost the
election, and died; but there, by the out-
rageous bay window, frescoed in pears,
apples and the serpents of the earthly
paradise, the good-hearted Señora Paquita
thought, in vain, to carry out her serene
old age, comforted by her wily needles and
the smile of posterity. But one day the

husbands of the daughters arrived (Brazilian sons-in-law), and, the mask having been ripped away, carried those good things off. Of the duenna, and of the others, not a word more was ever heard — one of the descendents came back later in one of the last wars and performed miracles, it is said. By then, however, it was, more or less, the time of the Tripolitan hymns. And these objects, these houses, stayed inside the living circle so long as it lasted. For few felt from the start that the cold was actually coming; and among these, perhaps, was my father who, even during the hottest days of August, supper out on the terrace over (carried on amidst moths and more persistent insects), and after having thrown a wool shawl around his shoulders, would repeat, always in French for who knows what reason, 'il fait bien froid, bien froid'; then he would go off immediately into his room and lie down on the bed and smoke his 7 centime Cavour.

VISIT TO FADIN

Past Madonna dell'Orto, then under the
galleries which run through the center of
town, I turned at last up the ramp which
led to the hospital, arriving soon afterward
where the patient had not been expect-
ing to see me: on the balcony with the
incurables, taking the sun. He caught
sight of me immediately, and didn't seem
at all surprised. He still had his hair cut

short, recently barbered; the face, how-
ever, was hollower, flushing red at the
cheekbones; the eyes, as beautiful as
before, were beginning to blear into a
deeper halo. I had come without warning,
and on a bad day: not even his Carlina,
'the angelic musician,' had been able to be
there.

The sea, below, was empty, and scattered
along the coast were the marzipan archi-
tectures of the newly rich.

Last stop of the voyage: many of your oc-
casional companions (workmen, clerks,
hairdressers) had already gone down
ahead of you, noiselessly, vanishing from
their beds. You had brought many books
with you, and had put them in the place
you used to reserve for your battered
knapsack: old books no longer in style;
except for one small volume of poetry that
I had taken once and that now will remain
with me, as we had then guessed without
saying so.

Of the conversation I remember nothing.

Certainly he didn't need to bring up any of the deeper matters, the universal ones, he who had always lived in a human way; that is to say, simply and silently. Exit Fadin. And to say now that you are no longer here is to say only that you have entered a different order of things, in that the one we move in here, we latecomers, as insane as it is, seems to our way of thinking the only one in which "god" can spread out all of his possibilities, become known and recognized within the framework of an assumption whose significance we do not understand. (Even he, then, would have need of us? If that's a blasphemy, well, it's certainly not our worst.)

Always to be among the first, and to *know*, this is what counts, even if the *why* of the play escapes us. He who has had from you this great lesson of *daily decency* (the most difficult of virtues) can wait without haste for the book of your relics. Your word, perhaps, was not among those that are written down.

IV

FLASHES AND DEDICATIONS

TOWARDS SIENA

How sad, that memory at its fullest
has no one to hold it back.

(The flight of pigs that night
on the Ambretta, the car bouncing, then fording the
    river;
then the carillon of San Gusmè;
and a May moon, all stains . . .)

The jack-in-the-box has sprung open
just where my God threw down his mask,
hurled lightning down on the rebel.

ON THE GREVE

Now a glance no longer sustains me
as once it did, when you would lean out at my whistle
and I could hardly see you.   A boulder, a deep, splayed
furrow, the black flight of a swallow,
a lid clamped on the cauldron of the world . . .

Bread to me is that velvet bud
which opens out to a mandolin's glissando,
water your rustle flowing;
your deep, deep breath is wine.

THE BLACK TROUT

Reading

Graduates in Economics,
Doctors of Divinity
bent over the evening water;
the trout nuzzles the surface and is gone.
Its carbonic flash
is a lock of your hair fish-tailing
in your bath, a sigh which rises
from the deep chambers of your office.

A METROPOLITAN CHRISTMAS
London

Mistletoe, from childhood a hanging cluster
of faith and hoar-frost over your washstand
and the oval mirror which your shepherd-curls
now shadow among the paper saints and photographs
of boys slipped helter-skelter into
the frame; an empty decanter,
small glasses of ashes and rinds,
the lights of Mayfair; then, at a crossroads,
souls and bottles which could not be opened —
no longer war or peace; the final whirr
of a pigeon unable to follow you
on the escalator which slides you down . . .

74

FREEING A 'DOVE'

Ely Cathedral

A white dove has come down to me
among pillars, under spires where the sky nests.
Dawns and lights, suspended; I have loved the sun,
the color of honey; now I ask for the dark,
I ask for the fire that smolders, this tomb
which does not fly, your look which dares it to.

ARGYLL TOUR

Glasgow

Children under the cedar tree, mushrooms or new
   mould
sprung up after the downpour;
the new foal in a cage
with the sign 'He Bites';
clouds of naphtha, suspended
over the walled canals;
smoke-puffs of gulls, odor of tallow
and dates, the lowing of the barges,
chains that slacken

               — but I was unaware of yours — ,

in the wake
leaps of tuna, sleep, long shrieks
of rats, obscene laughter, before you
appeared to your slave . . .

WIND ON THE CRESCENT

Edinburgh

The big bridge did not lead to you.
I would have reached you even by sailing
the sewer sluices, at your command.   But
my strength, with the sun on the veranda
windows, already was slipping, wearing thin.

The man preaching on the Crescent
asked me 'Do you know where God is?'   I knew
and I told him.   He shook his head and disappeared
in the whirlwind which gathered men and houses
and lifted them up, into the darkness.

ON THE HIGHEST COLUMN
Mosque of Damascus

He will have to get up there,
Christ the judge,
to say his word.
Among the gravel of the seven shingled river beds,
crows and blackcaps,
nettles and sunflowers
will humble themselves together.

But in that twilight it was you on the summit:

shadowed, wings matted, crippled
from the ice of Antilibano; and still
your lightning changed the black diadems
of stumps into bird-lime; the Column
spelled out the Law only for you.

TOWARDS FINISTERRE

With the bellowing of the stags in the Breton rain,
the arc of your eyelash was quenched
in the first darkening to filter later
onto the dawn-washed plaster sky where bicycle wheels,
spindles, spokes and fringes of shaking trees whirl.
Perhaps I have no other proof that God sees me,
that your eyes, circles of aquamarine, still look for him.

ON THE LLOBREGAT

From the incorruptible green of the camphor tree
two notes, an interval of a major third.
The cuckoo, not the screech-owl, I told you; but in
     the meantime, with a jerk,
you had jammed down the accelerator.

FROM THE TRAIN

The solferino ring-neck turtle doves
are at Sesto Calende for the first time
in man's memory. So the newspapers
announce. Face pressed to the window,
I looked for them in vain. A collar of yours,
yes, but of another color, bent over the top
of a reed, disintegrating. It flashed
only for me, falling into a pond. And their rush
of fire blinded me to the other.

SYRIA

The ancients said that poetry
is a stairway to God.   Maybe it isn't so
if you read me.   But I knew it the day
that I found the voice for you again, loosed
in a flock of clouds and goats
bursting out of a ravine to browse the slaver
of thorn and bulrush; the lean faces
of the moon and sun became one face,
the car was broken down and an arrow
of blood on a boulder pointed
the way to Aleppo.

WINTER LIGHT

When I came down from the sky of Palmyra
to dwarf palms and the candied, ruined temples
and a scratch on the throat warned me
you would have carried me off;
when I came down from the sky of the Acropolis
and found, for kilometers, baskets
of octopus and moray eels
(the saw of those teeth
on the shrunken heart!);

when I left the summits of the inhuman dawns
for the cold museum
of mummies and scarabs (you were sick,
my only life) and confronted pumice
and jasper, the sun and the sand, the mud
and the holy clay —
                    at the spark
which rose, I became new, burned to ashes.

FOR AN 'HOMAGE TO RIMBAUD'

Late-comer from the cocoon, marvellous
butterfly who from a lectern
deflowers the exile of Charleville,
O do not follow him in his frenzied
partridge-like flight, do not scatter
broken feathers, gardenia petals
on the black ice of the asphalt! Your flight
will be more terrible if risen
from these wings of pollen and silk
into the scarlet halo in which you believe,
daughter of the sun, handmaiden of his first
thought and now, up there, his mistress

SPELLBOUND

O stay closed and free in the islands
of your thought and mine,
in the buoyant flame which surrounds you
and which I did not know before
meeting Diotima,
she who so resembled you!
In her the amorous cicada vibrates louder
in the cherry tree of your garden.
Around, the world tightens; incandescent,
in the lava which brings to Galilee
your earthly love, you wait for the hour
to discover that veil which one day
betrothed you to your God.

V

SILVAE

IRIS

When all at once St. Martin* dumps
his burning coals and shoves them deep down into the
   dark craw
of Ontario's furnace;
the snapping of pine cones among the embers,
the smoke of steeped poppies,
the blood-smeared Face on the shroud
that drops between me and you:
*Indian Summer

               this and little else (if a sign
or wink from you *can* be a little thing in the wrestling
that forces me now into this charnel house, back
to the wall, where sky-blue sapphires
and palms fronds and storks on one leg still don't shut
     out
the sickening view from this poor
wandering Nestorian)

               is as much of you as washes up from the
                         shipwreck
of my people, of yours, now that this fire
of frost calls to mind your land
that you never saw; and I have
no other rosary between my fingers; no other flame
but this one, fashioned of resin and berries,
has covered you.

*   *   *

Others' hearts are not your heart;
the lynx has a different smile than the tame house cat
waiting in ambush for the hummingbird in the laurel;
but you might think them alike if you ventured
out of the shade of the sycamore;
or is it, perhaps, that mask on the white cloth,
that purple effigy, which has guided you?

92

So your work (which is a form
of His) might flower in other lights,
Iris of Canaan, you faded away
in the nimbus of mistletoe and butcher's broom
that your heart guides
through the world's night, beyond the mirage
of desert blooms, your brothers.

If you appear, you carry me back here, under the
    pergola
of stripped vines, beside the pier
of our river — and the ferry doesn't turn back,
and the sun of St. Martin melts, and goes black.
But if you return, you are no longer you,
your earthly legend is changed, you don't wait
for the prow at the landing,
you have no further glances, no yesterdays, no
    tomorrows;
because His work (transformed
into yours) *must be carried on.*

IN THE GREENHOUSE

The lemon bushes overflowed
with the patter of mole paws,
the scythe shined
in its rosary of cautious water drops.

A dot, a ladybug,
ignited upon the quince berries
as the snort of a rearing pony broke through,
bored with his rub-down — then the dream took over.

Kidnapped, and weightless, I was drenched
with you, your outline
was my hidden breath, your face
merged with my face, and the dark

idea of God descended
upon the living few, amid heavenly
sounds, amid childish drums,
amid suspended globes of lightning

upon me, upon you, and over the lemons . . .

IN THE PARK

In the shade of the magnolia
which grows always smaller and smaller
there comes a 'whoosh' from the blow gun
and the dart grazes me and is lost.

It seemed a fallen leaf
from the poplar which, in a gust of wind,
changes color, dwindles away — perhaps a hand
come down from the distance through the foliage.

A laugh that doesn't belong to me
bores into the grizzled branches
right up to my chest, shaking from it
a trilling that rattles my veins,

and I laugh with you on the warped
wheel of the shade, I stretch out,
freed from myself, on the bony
roots which jut out and I batter

your face with wisps of straw . . .

THE ORCHARD

I don't know, sweet messenger
come down, favorite
of my God (perhaps, even, of yours), if in the grove
of the medlar trees where the nesting wrens
moan, weakening out in the evening;
I don't know if in the garden
where the acorns sleet down and, over the wall,
the air-colored hornbeam garlands unravel,
marking the foamy edge of the breakers, a veil

among the crowns of rock
now overrun, now black black, now glittering more
than the first star that oozes through —

I don't know if your muffled step
in the blind nightmare where I have been growing
toward death since the day I first saw you;
I don't know if your footfall, which makes my veins
    beat,
should it come closer in this tangling,
is the one that took me that other summer
before the gust of wind,
grazing against the raw peak of the Mesco,
broke up my mirror; —
I don't know if the hand that touches my shoulder
is the same one that once
answered, on the clavichord, the moans
from other nests, from other thickets now burned.

The hour of torture, the hour of moaning
that fell upon the world;
the hour that you saw coming as clearly as if you had
    read it in a book,
freezing your crystalline stare
right to the bottom of things, there where the curtains
    acrid
with soot, raised over the fitful flashings

from workshops, hid Vulcan's hammer
from sight;
the Day of Wrath which, over and over, the cock
announced to the perjured
did not cut you off, indivisible soul,
from its almost inhuman pain, did not melt you
in the bowl of fire, O heart of amethyst.

O silent lips, parched from the long journey
down the pathway of air
which bore you along, O limbs that I can hardly
tell from my own, O fingers that quench
the thirst of the dead, and the living that burn,
O design that you have made (outside your own
    measurements),
the hands of the quadrant, expanding yourself
into man-time, into man-space, into furies
of incarnate demons, onto the foreheads of angels
swooping downward . . . If the power
that turns the record *already cut* was another,
surely your destiny joined to mine
would find a single groove.

BEACH AT VERSILIA

I pray for my dead so that they might pray
for me, for my living, as I ask for them
not resurrection but, instead, the fulfillment
of that life they have had
unexplained, and unexplainable; today,
they rarely descend from the open horizons
when riots of water and sky open
windows to the tentacles of the evening — less and less
    often
a cutter, the sky-hung goshawk, white-crested,
white-pinioned, brings them to the sand.

Beds of zinnias dyed like wax flowers
(grandmothers with stiff, chin-strapped bonnets water
    them,
refusing to glance at anyone from the outside street
who won't surrender his sickness
into their unpitying hands); courtyards of grizzled,
    trellised
vines where angry voices
forbid left-overs to the friar-colored cat
if he dare enter; rubble and flat overlooks
on low houses along an undulating
descent of dunes, and umbrellas opened
against a grey sun; sand that can't nourish
the trees sacred to my childhood, the wild pine,
the fig and the eucalyptus.

In that shade my early years were crowded,
heavy with honey, so long abandoned;
in that shade, often spread out under
only two strips of crepe-paper riddled
with mosquitos, I slept — there, in the corner room,
next to the kitchen, at nighttime;
in the deeps of siestas
while cicadas jangled, dazzling in my sleep,
I sometimes would catch a glimpse, over the wall,
    at the wash-basin,
of the shadows of loved ones massaging the moray eels,

forcing the bones back to the tails, then cutting them
   out;
in that endless high humming
others now gone, with rakes and shears
would leave the nursery
of dwarf stalks for the burnt
evergreens, for the channels greedy for water.

Those years of cliffs and closed horizons
were custodians of lives still human,
of acts still understandable — like the breathing,
like the final sigh of underwater creatures
then similar to man, or close to him
even in name: the priest fish, the swallow fish,
the lobster — wolf of the trap — who
forgets his pinchers when Alice
comes near . . . and the trapeze acts
of familiar mice from one palm tree
to the other — time that once was measurable
until this endless sea opened,
this sea of clay and washed-up refuse.

EZEKIEL SAW THE WHEEL

Strange hand, have you snatched me away
from the tangles of ivy?
I was leaning against the clammy
basin, the air was black,
only one vein of onyx throbbed
in the distance, some stalk in the storm.
But the hand did not loosen,
in the darkness its grip hardened toward ice,
and the rain that dissolved
in my hair, and in your hair then,
too slight, too smooth,

ferreted around tenaciously for the sign
long buried inside me by the mound of earth,
by the mountain of sand I had in my heart
stored up against my next attempt
to choke off your voice,
to push it down into the brief circle
that transforms everything —
it rasped and cracked, its fragments drifting out
into the open where slipper prints
gathered on hardened mud,
where the splinter of your cross
in festering pulp of old
and rotting beams thickened, where the smile,
skull-like, that came between us tightened
as the threatening Wheel appeared
among the stalactites of dawn
and the bloodied petals of the peach tree
fell over me,
and with them
your grasp . . . like now.

HITLER SPRING

Né quella ch'a veder lo sol si gira . . . *(Dante (?) to Giovanni Quirini)*

A snowfall of maddened moths
swirls from the parapets, thickening in the street lamps,
dropping a sheet upon the ground
which crackles like sugar underfoot; the almost-summer
    air
sets free now the night-frost
it held in the secret pits of the dead season,
in the orchards of Maiano washing open trenches of
    sand.

A moment ago a hell-bent messenger
roared past us, cheered on by his henchmen;
a mystic gulf, lighted and hung with swastikas, grabbed
    him,

and gulped him down.
                              The poor and harmless shop
    windows
are closed, though they, too, are armed
with cannon and toys of war;
the butcher has clanged down his iron curtain —
once he would have decorated the goats' heads
that hung on his hooks with the new, wild berries;
those were the mild blood-lettings, rituals, even,
for amateur killers whose slaughter now has been
    transformed
into a foul jangle of broken wings,
of larva upon the mudbanks, of water
that goes on gnawing into the pilings, and no one, now,
no one is guiltless.

Is it all for nothing then? — and the swoosh of the
    roman candles
on St. John's Day, sadly white-washing on the
    horizon; the vows
and the long farewells, binding as baptisms
in the mournful waiting for the hordes
(diamond dust powdered the air,
shook down on the glaciers and rivers of your beaches
the seven burning angels of Tobias, the widening seed
of the future); and the heliotropes unfolding
from your fingers — all cindered, sucked dry

by a driving pollen that jars like fire,
that is toothed like a blizzard . . .

        Spring's re-opened wound
is welcome if it can refreeze this other death! Look up,
Clizia, it is your destiny; you,
whom unchanging love preserves transformed —
at least until the blind sun you carry inside you
is dazzled by that other, is destroyed
in Him for each of us. Perhaps the sirens, the tolling
   bells
that call to the monsters in the twilight
of their Pandemonium already are mixing
with the sound that, unloosed from above, descends,
   and conquers —
with the breath of a dawn that tomorrow
may come once more to each of us, white,
but lacking the terrifying wings,
         in the raw and shingled gulches of the south . . .

VOICE ARRIVING WITH THE COOTS

Since the road already travelled, if I turned back,
is longer than the goat path that takes me now
to where we shall melt like wax,
and the bloomed weeds don't soothe the heart,
but only their own twigs and the blood of cemeteries,
here you are, father, outside
the dark that held you back, erect in the light's glare,
without shawl or beret, in the dull shudder
which spoke out once in the dawn,

announcing the miners' barges half-sunk
from their great loads, black on the high waves.

The shadow that follows me, father,
to your grave, alert,
leans on a bust of Hermes, and has a proud
toss of the head that pushes back
from the forehead, from the burning eyes and thick
  eyebrows,
her childish wave of hair;
this shadow weighs no more than you do, father,
so long buried now — the first sun's rays
of the day transfix her, jerky
butterflies drift over her, a mimosa
brushes against her, and does not scare.

The faithful shadow and the dumb one rising up,
the one who disembodied the inner fire
and the one whom long years in another time
(hard years for me) have stripped of flesh,
talk together, words which I, stock-still
on the edge of understanding, cannot hear. The one,
  perhaps,
will find again the order wherein love burned
for Him who moved her, and not for herself;
but the other is terrified and fears
that the warm ghost of a memory that he remains
to his sons will soon grow cold, and disappear.

"I have thought of you, I have remembered
for everyone. Now you return to the open sky
that changes you. This cliff-line
still tempts you? Yes, the wave-reach is the same
as it always was, the sea that joins you
to my earlier beaches, when I still had wings, does
    not dissolve.
Calling to mind those shores, I
have arrived with the coots
to take you away from yours. Memory
isn't a sin so long as it does some good.
After that it's like the slow-wittedness of moles,
servility gone stale, and green with mold . . ."

                    The wind of the day
mingles the live shadow and the other one
still holding back in a middle ground, a ground that
    thrusts away
my hands, and breaks my breath
in my full lungs, in the ditch
enclosing the start of memory.
Thus it slackens, before it can lock
onto the images, onto the words, onto the dark
remembering senses of the past, the emptiness
we once occupied which awaits us again, when it is time
to take us back, to take us in.

THE SHADOW OF THE MAGNOLIA

The shadow of the Japanese magnolia
drapes thinner, bonier fingers over the ground now
that its purple blooms are gone. A cicada drums,
at intervals, overhead. It is no longer,
Clizia, a season of singing in unison, a time
when the limitless god devours his faithful, then gives
    them back their blood.

Giving up was easier, dying
at the first flurry of wings, at the first
hand-lock with the enemy — child's play.
A harder life begins now: but not you,
wasted away by sunlight, rooted in the earth — yet still
a delicate thrush who flies high over the hoarfrost
of your river banks; not you, frail fugitive
for whom zenith, nadir, Cancer and Capricorn
remain unfocused, so that the war might be
inside you and inside him who adores
on you the stigmata of your Bridegroom;
you are not jarred by the stutter and shiver of sleet . . .
Others withdraw and give way.   The carver's file,
once subtle and true, will be silent, the hollow hull
of the singer will soon be powdered glass
under your feet, the shadow dulls like a bruise —
it's autumn, it's winter, it's the other side of the sky
that leads you on. There I swim, break water,
a fish in the high dry air under the new moon.

                                        Addio.

THE LEMON-YELLOW ROOSTER

There, where you fall after the shot is fired
(your voice boils up again, reddish-black
ragout of heaven and earth over a low flame),
I also plane down, I also burn in the same ditch.

Someone sobbing cries for help. It was far sweeter
to live than to sink down to the bottom of this mess,
far easier to waste away in the wind than
here in this foul, encrusted slime over the flame.

I feel your wound in my breast, under
the clotted wings; in my lumbering flight

I try a wall, and now all that is left of us
is a few feathers on the frosted ilex bush.

A scramble of nests, loves, nests
with marbled eggs, divinities! Now the star
of the jasmine plant shines in the darkness . . .
like a maggot.   And Zeus is buried.

THE EEL

The eel, siren
of the cold seas, who leaves her Baltic playground
for our warm waters, our estuaries,
our rivers, who cuts through their deepest soundings,
against their angry tides, from branch to branch,
from stem to stem as they thin,
farther and farther inward, snaking
into the heart of the rocky landscape, worming
through the arteries of slime until one day
a blaze, struck from the chestnut blossoms,
flares her tracks through the pools of dead water,

in the ruts cut out of the cliffs
which fall away from the Apennines to the Romagna;
the eel, whiplash, twisting torch,
love's arrow on earth, which only
our gullies and dried-out, burned-out streams
can lead to the paradises of fecundity;
green spirit that hunts for life
only there, where drought and desolation gnaw,
a spark that says everything starts
where everything is charred, stumps buried;
vanishing rainbow, twin sister
to her you set behind your own cyclids
and let shine out over the sons of men, on us
up to our hairlines in your breathing mud . . .
and *you* can't call her sister?

VI

PRIVATE MADRIGALS

THE PROCESSIONS OF 1949

Sultry lightning along the points of departure,
an ashen, fog-shut leaving
followed by halos which weren't any better; a rumbling
of wheels, the naggings on the very first
risings of the hill;
a vomiting, a stench infecting
the turf for us, the marching devotees,

      . . . if it weren't
for that dump-heap of yours *in vitro*, in the scummy
  conduit,

among the soap bubbles and heavy insects.

Who lies more, who laments?   It was your moment
    forever;
it is whenever you come on.
Your furious, angelic virtue
put to flight with a glove the saintly
pilgrims, Cybele and the Corybants.

MAGENTA-COLORED CLOUDS . . .

Magenta-colored clouds thickened
in the cave of Fingal across the water
when I said, "pump harder,
sweetheart," and with a jerk
the tandem churned out of the mud
and picked up speed through the barriers of the
   embankment.

Copper-colored clouds draped
like bridges over the church spires of Agliena,
over the rusty moors when
I said, "stop!," and your ebony wing

took up the whole horizon
with its long, unbearable shuddering.

Like Pafnuzio in the desert, I wanted
too much to conquer you, and so was conquered.
I fly. I stay with you;
to die, to live, is all one lump, a knot dyed
by your own color, and hot from the cave's breath,
deep, and barely audible.

FOR AN ALBUM

I started, in fact, this morning
tossing the hook out for you.
But no tail squirmed, no fin flickered,
in the murky pools,
no wind came down from the hills of Monferrini
with your scent on it.
I went on with my day
continually looking for you, larva, tadpole,
wisp of creeper, ptarmigan,
gazelle, zebu, okapi,
black cloud, hail

before the harvest: I gleaned
even among the drenched vine rows without finding
   a trace of you.
I kept at it until late in the evening
without knowing that three small boxes
— SAND, SODA, SOAP, the pigeon-roost
from which your escape began: from a kitchen, —
would have opened for me at my touch.
Thus you vanished down the indefinite horizon.
There isn't the vaguest thought that you lock up the
   lightning,
but he who has seen the light won't give it up.
I stretched out under your cherry tree — I was
already too rich to keep you alive.

FROM A SWISS LAKE

My little fox, at one time I, too,
was the "assassinated poet": there in the hazelnut
    grove
razed by the bonfire, cave-like
in that lair, a circle like strung sequins
ignited your face, then lowered slowly
along its way until it touched
the smoke, and disappeared; and I, anxiously,
called for the end of that dark
emblem of your uncaged life, bitter,
atrociously fragile, yet strong.

Is it you who shines in the darkness? I enter
the pulsing furrow of night on a sizzling pathway,

hot on the trail of your light
predator's tracks (a mark
almost invisible, star-shaped), and tumble,
I, outsider; suddenly a black duck
beats upward on the clotted air from far out on the lake;
he leads the way to the new fire, where he will burn.

ANNIVERSARY

From the time of your birth,
little fox, I have been on my knees.
From that day on I have felt the war
with evil won, my sins atoned for.

A flame was burning and burning; onto your roof,
onto mine, I saw the terror overflow.
You grew like a young stalk; and I, in the coolness
of battle lulls, spied on that growing up.

I stay on my knees: the gift that I dreamed of,
not for me but for everyone,
belongs now only to me, with God divided
from men, from the blood clotted and crisp
on the high branches, on the fruit.

VII
TEMPORARY CONCLUSIONS

LITTLE TESTAMENT

This light that flashes in the night
of my mind's skull,
this mother-of-pearl snail's track,
this emery board of ground-up glass,
is not the glow from any church or factory
that might sustain the clerical red, or black.
I have only this iris
to leave you, testimony
of a faith too often fought for,
of a hope that burned slower
than a green log on a fire.

Keep its dust in your compact
when every light goes out,
and the sardana becomes infernal
and Lucifer's shade rises upon some boat bow
in the Thames or Hudson or Seine,
turning his coal-black wings
half cut away by weariness, and tells you, "Now."
It's no inheritance, no goodluck piece
to pacify those monsoons
along the spider's thread of memory;
anyone's biography survives
only in its own ashes,
and persistence is nothing but extinction.
The sign was a just one: whoever has seen it
cannot but find you again.
Each knows his own: pride
was never escape, humility
never a cowardice; that tenuous glow down there
was more than just a match.

THE PRISONER'S DREAM

Here dawns and twilights differ merely by motions:

The zigzag of plane formations over the watch-tower
when the fighting comes closer, my only wings;
the needles of arctic air;
the eye of the turnkey at the peephole;
the crack of nuts being shelled; oily
hissings and sputters from the kitchens, real
or imagined roasting spits — but the straw is gold,
the wine-red lantern is a fireplace
if at night I dream I'm at your feet.

The purging goes on as it always has — without a
      reason.
They say that whoever gives in, and signs,
can save himself from the executions, these killings

methodical as the slaughter of geese;
that whoever breaks, turns stoolie,
state's witness, and denounces everything in sight,
will grab the serving spoon
instead of being on it in the *pâté*,
food for the guts of tin gods.

Slow-witted and sluggish, ulcerated
by this mattress that pricks my skin like wire-ends,
I am no different than the moth wings
my shoes keep powdering to dust on the tiles,
than the iridescent kimonos of light
that hang like washing from the battlements at dawn;
I have smelled on the wind the odor
of sweet cakes from the ovens,
I have looked around, I have conjured
rainbows on the spider-webbed horizons,
conjured flowers with cell bars for a trellis;
I have risen up only to fall again
into this ditch where every century is a minute —
and the blows go on, over and over . . . and the
    footsteps;
and still I don't know, when the banquet is finally
    served,
if I shall be the eater or the eaten. The wait is long;
my dream of you is not yet over.

NOTES

This book contains a selection of the poems I have written since *The Occasions*. The first part republishes *Finisterre* (poems from 1940-1942) as the book appeared (1943) in the series Collana di Lugano, edited by Pino Bernasconi A second edition of the book, published in Florence by Barbera, and edited by Giorgio Zampa, contained two prose pieces and three additional poems that will be found in the second and fifth sections of the present volume. The notes that follow here are taken in part from the Florentine edition of *Finisterre*; and in part they are new.

Two in Twilight. It was published in May 1943 with this notation: "In the old workbook where I found, two years ago, *Dora Markus*, there were also these notes and lines that were dated 5 September 1926. I recopied them, adding a title a bit Browningesque (*Two in the Campagna*) and inserting a few words where there were blank spaces or crossings out. I also took out two useless lines. I did, that is, the work I should have done before if I had thought then that the rough draft would have still interested me after many years."

Visit to Fadin. Sergio Fadin. His Elegies were issued posthumously (with a preface by Sergio Solmi) by Vanni Scheiwiller, Milan, 1943.

Where the Tennis Court Was . . . It's from 1943 also. *Del Salon* etc: from *Rimas* by Becquer.

Florentine Madrigals. A Bedlington (terrier), therefore a dog, and not an airplane, as has been believed, stuck his face out from one of the abutments of Santa Trinita bridge one dawn during those days. The gong is an echo of the one used to call the family to table. (But the family is no longer there.) The magnesium lamp and the dedications (fourth section) belong to the years 1948-1952. The *Silvae* (excluding *Iris*, which is from 1946) were written between 1944 and 1950. The *Madrigals* are later (excluding *The Processions of 1949*).

Flashes and Dedications. Freeing a 'Dove'. The Dove was a type of tourist airplane built in those days (1948). *Argyll Tour*: a boat tour around the environs of Glasgow. *Wind on the Crescent*: several streets that half-way encircle Glasgow are called halfmoons or crescents. *On the Llobregat*: the Llobregat is a river one comes on between Barcelona and Monserrat.

Silvae. Iris: the person is the same one as in *The Red Lily* and in all the poems in *Finisterre*. She returns in the *Hitler Spring*, in various poems of the *Silvae* section (also with the name Clizia) and in the *Little Testament*. She has already appeared in many of the poems in *The Occasions*: especially in the *Motets* and *New Stanzas*. *Iris* is a poem I dreamed and then translated from a non-existent language: I am perhaps more its "medium" than its author. Another is the figure in *Ballad Written in a Clinic*, another still that of the *Flashes and Dedications* and the *Madrigals*.

The *Hitler Spring*.   Hitler and Mussolini in Florence. Gala evening at the Communal Theater.   On the Arno, a snowfall of white butterflies.

The *Little Testament* is from 12 May 1953.   The *Prisoner's Dream* was published in Calamandrei's *Ponte* (No. 10, October 1954).   In this same magazine, years earlier, the *Ballad* was published.